WELCOME TO MERIDEE WINTERS CHORD QUEST

Our brains are wired to learn by patterns – finally, a music book series that teaches that way (AND sure has fun doing it).

Welcome to Chord Quest – a kids' version of Meridee's cult-favorite Chord Crash Course series, which teaches key skills like chords, patterns, transposition, lead sheet reading and much, much more. Known for its playful comic-book design and trailblazing "learn by pattern and shape" approach, one of Chord Quest's most unique features is that it doesn't require you to read music. (Which is why students can learn chord progressions within just a few minutes and their favorite songs within just a few chapters.)

Here in book two you'll portal from chapter to chapter as you learn skills, earn powers, play great music and work your way to a final challenge. (You'll also save creativity, take down the Baron von Boring and destroy a factory while you're at it.)

Psst! Are you a student of our All Star Piano Patterns Series? Chord Quest is a re-imagined reboot of those books. You can pick up right where you left off!

IN CHORD QUEST LEVEL 2, YOU'LL LEARN:

- ★ Hands-together Arpeggio Patterns
- ★ Transposition
- ★ Lead Sheet Reading
- ★ New Rhythms
- ★ Alberti and Oom-pah Patterns
- ★ Songwriting
- ★ Famous Progressions
- ★ Four Chord Concert
- ★ And more!

Head to mwfunstuff.com/cq2 for fun extras, online lesson info and more!

This book is a great standalone tool - OR an awesome finger exercise book to supplement any method!

EVIL VILLAIN

YOU DON'T HAVE TO READ MUSIC. WE'RE SERIOUS.

The ability to read music is an incredible skill, and we're all for it. (Our Note Quest Game Book was created to specifically build that skill.) The Chord Quest series is designed to work for all levels, however, including those who can and can't read music. Music, including chords and arpeggios, is largely a beautiful combination of patterns. By learning and applying these patterns, anyone can play and write music. For those who can read music, this book works as a great supplement, adding higher level chord theory and comping skills to your existing skill set.

EXCLUSIVE TO THE MERIDEE WINTERS UNIVERSE

These tools will help you on your musical adventure:

KINESTHETIC KEYBOARDS will show you what to play.

QUANTUM QUIZZES will solidify what you've learned.

TRANSPOSITION SONGWRITING
SKILL BADGES will be earned each chapter.

THE LAB will give you a chance to experiment and create.

CHORD QUEST POWERFUL PIANO LESSONS
LEVEL 2: EASY KEYBOARD PATTERNS FOR KIDS

CHAPTER 1: REVIEW
Arpeggios .... (pg. 2)
 1. Arpeggio Sonic Scale .... (pg. 2)
Chords .... (pg. 3)
 2. Cosmic Chord Climb .... (pg. 3)
Intervals: 2nds, 3rds, 4ths .... (pg. 4)
 3. Interstellar Interval Review.......... (pg. 4)
Intervals: 5ths .... (pg. 5)
 4. Far-Out Fifths Review .... (pg. 5)
Major and Minor Chords .... (pg. 6)
 5. Major to Minor .... (pg. 7)
Root Notes and Chord Symbols .... (pg. 8)
 6. Chord Symbol Crash Landing.......... (pg. 8)
Chord Progressions .... (pg. 9)
 7. Modal Meteor Progression Review..... (pg. 9)
Quantum Quiz .... (pg. 10)

CHAPTER 2: ASTRO ARPEGGIOS
 8. Double Star Arpeggio Scale........... (pg. 12)
 9. Cosmic Combo .... (pg. 13)
A "Tail" of Two Comets .... (pg. 14)
 10. A Section: Double Arpeggio .... (pg. 14)
 11. B Section: Arpeggio, Chord .... (pg. 15)
 12. C Section: Chord, Arpeggio .... (pg. 15)
 13. Rock The Scale .... (pg. 17)
 14. Scale The Rock .... (pg. 17)
 15. Black Hole Ballad - A Section .... (pg. 18)
 16. Black Hole Ballad - B Section .... (pg. 18)
 17. Black Hole Ballad - C Section .... (pg. 19)
Let's Experiment! .... (pg. 20)
Quantum Quiz .... (pg. 22)

CHAPTER 3: TRANSPOSITION
Top Reasons to Transpose .... (pg. 24)
Mission: Transposition .... (pg. 25)
Tackling Transposition .... (pg. 26)
Let's Look at Chord Scales .... (pg. 27)
Transposing in 4 steps .... (pg. 28)
Practice Transposing .... (pg. 29)
Transposing Pachelbel .... (pg. 30)
 18. Pachelbel's Canon in C .... (pg. 30)
 19. Pachelbel's Canon in C, Style 2 .... (pg. 30)
 20. Pachelbel's Canon in D .... (pg. 31)
 21. Pachelbel's Canon in D, Style 2 .... (pg. 31)
Quantum Quiz .... (pg. 32)

CHAPTER 4: OOM-PAH
Oom-Pah-Pah Waltzes .... (pg. 34)
 22. Celestial Circus .... (pg. 34)
 23. Waltz of Whimsy .... (pg. 35)
 24. Transposition Trapeze .... (pg. 35)
 25. Oom-Pah Oom-Pah .... (pg. 36)
 26. Oom-Pah Doo Wop .... (pg. 37)
 27. Klezmerized .... (pg. 39)
 28. Andalusian Arpeggios .... (pg. 40)
 29. Andalusian Oom-Pah .... (pg. 40)
 30. Andalusian Root Fifth Pattern ...... (pg. 41)
Quantum Quiz .... (pg. 42)

CHAPTER 5: RHYTHM RUMBLE
Bring In The Bass .... (pg. 44)
 31. Feel The Beat .... (pg. 44)
 32. Drive The Beat .... (pg. 45)
 33. Move It .... (pg. 46)
 34. Groove It .... (pg. 47)
 35. Face The Fifths .... (pg. 48)
 36. Fifths Rock .... (pg. 49)
 37. Chord Rock in C Major .... (pg. 50)
 38. Transpose: Chord Rock in G Major ... (pg. 51)
 39. Transpose: Chord Rock in D Major ... (pg. 51)
Quantum Quiz .... (pg. 52)

CHAPTER 6: SUPER SKILL: LEAD SHEETS
How Do You Play A Lead Sheet? .... (pg. 54)
Cover Songs: Online Tools .... (pg. 56)
Quantum Quiz .... (pg. 58)

CHAPTER 7: ALBERTI BASS

How Do You Play Alberti Bass? . . . . (pg. 60)
40. Alberti Scale Number 1 . . . . (pg. 61)
41. Alberti Scale Number 2 . . . . (pg. 61)
42. Full Moon Fantasia - A Section . . . . (pg. 62)
43. Full Moon Fantasia - B Section . . . . (pg. 62)
44. Full Moon Fantasia - C Section . . . . (pg. 63)
45. Pachelbel's Canon - Variation 1 . . . . (pg. 64)
46. Pachelbel's Canon - Variation 2 . . . . (pg. 64)
47. Pachelbel's Canon - Variation 3 . . . . (pg. 65)
Quantum Quiz . . . . (pg. 66)

CHORD QUEST TEST

Reflections & Test Questions . . . . (pg. 76)
Songwriting Lab . . . . (pg. 78)
Write Down Your Creations! . . . . (pg. 80)
Chord Scale Glossary . . . . (pg. 82)
Chord Quest Award . . . . (pg. 84)

CHAPTER 8: UNIVERSAL CHORD CONCERT

Four Chord Concert . . . . (pg. 68)
48. Melodic Fifths . . . . (pg. 68)
49. Bottom Middle Top Middle . . . . (pg. 69)
50. Half Note Chords . . . . (pg. 69)
51. Pulse 1 . . . . (pg. 70)
52. Pulse 2 . . . . (pg. 70)
53. Pulse 3 . . . . (pg. 71)
54. Pulse 4 . . . . (pg. 71)
55. Melodic and Harmonic Fifths . . . . (pg. 71)
Best Set List in the Universe! . . . . (pg. 72)
Create Your Own Lyrics . . . . (pg. 73)
Quantum Quiz . . . . (pg. 74)

SNEAK PEEK: CHORD QUEST POWERFUL PIANO LESSONS LEVEL 3 (pg. 86)

MERIDEE WINTERS™

CHORD QUEST POWERFUL PIANO LESSONS LEVEL 2
EASY KEYBOARD PATTERNS FOR KIDS

Copyright 2012, 2019, 2020 by Meridee Winters. All rights reserved.
Music compositions © 2003, 2012, 2019, 2020 by Meridee Winters. All rights reserved.

Meridee Winters Publishing • 63 W. Lancaster Ave., Suite 7 • Ardmore, PA 19003
www.MerideeWintersMusicMethod.com
ISBN: 978-1-943821-66-2

Meridee Winters: Music Composer, Author, and Art Director
Kate Capps: Editor, Creative Consultant, Music Engraving
Sean Miller: Layout and Graphic Design, Additional Illustrations
Tatiana Tsitsura: Additional Design
Madé Dimas Wirawan: Illustrations
Armand Alidio: Cover Design, Additional Illustrations, Additional Design
Krysta Bernhardt: Additional Design
Gabriel Rhopers: Creative Consultant; Kaitlin Borden, Emily Cooley & Peter Horst: Proofreading

CHAPTER 1: REVIEW

Welcome to Chord Quest Level 2! For this quest, you'll journey across Planet Sunstone, portaling from chapter to chapter while learning skills and earning powers. Then you'll use these creative and musical powers to defeat the Baron von Boring. (We defeated Professor Perfecto in Chord Quest 1, but the forces of Blah are still at work. Now their plan is to make music BORING through the Baron von Boring's music books!) Luckily - you have a musical secret weapon: playing by shape and pattern (whether you can read music or not)!

Before jumping into the next quest, it's important that you review the core moves and concepts from the last book. If you're starting your Chord Quest adventure with this book, this chapter will fill you in. If you just completed Chord Quest Level 1, you may find this review to be a breeze. Go on, get started... and good luck!

REVIEW: ARPEGGIOS

Practice playing an arpeggio with your left hand… and then your right hand.

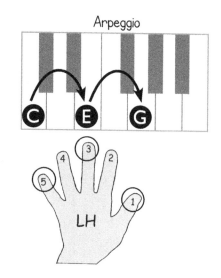
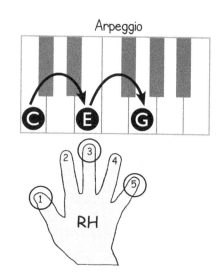

1. ARPEGGIO SONIC SCALE

Just play the shape! You don't need to read!

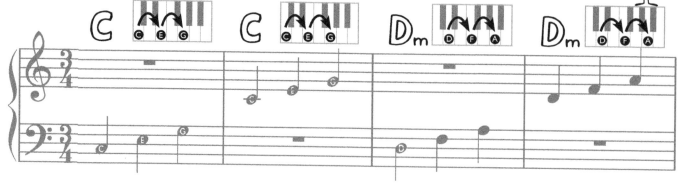

Keep going up!

REVIEW: CHORDS

Practice playing a chord with your left hand... and then your right hand.

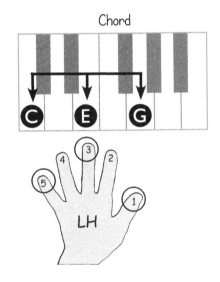
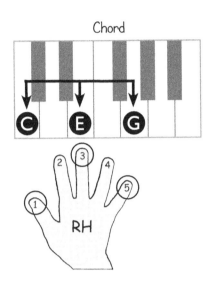

② COSMIC CHORD CLIMB

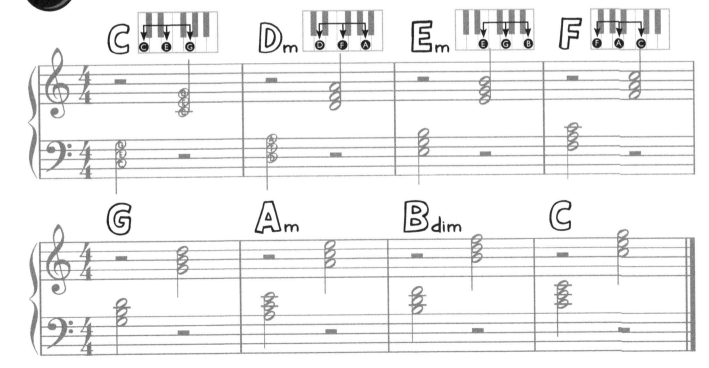

INTERVALS: 2NDS, 3RDS, 4THS

PRACTICE PLAYING A SECOND
(both melodic and harmonic)

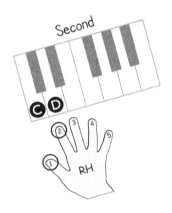

PRACTICE PLAYING A THIRD
(both melodic and harmonic)

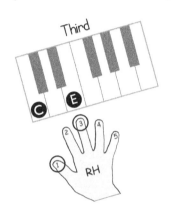

PRACTICE PLAYING A FOURTH
(both melodic and harmonic)

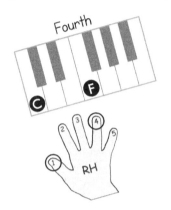

③ INTERSTELLAR INTERVAL REVIEW

Left hand stays on C while the right hand plays seconds, thirds and fourths.

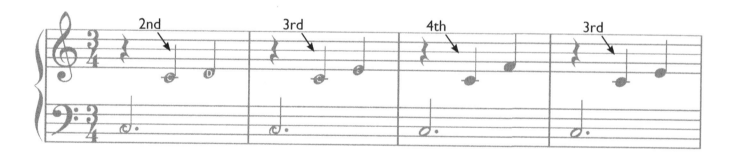

Review

INTERVALS: 5THS

Practice playing melodic fifths with your left hand.

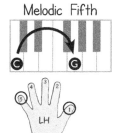

Practice playing melodic fifths with your right hand.

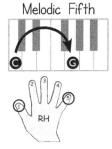

Practice playing harmonic fifths with your left hand.

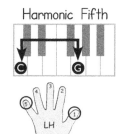

Practice playing harmonic fifths with your right hand.

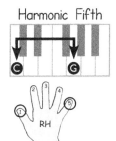

 FAR-OUT FIFTHS REVIEW

Left hand plays a harmonic fifth and the right hand answers with a melodic fifth.

Review

REVIEW: MAJOR AND MINOR CHORDS

WHAT IS A MAJOR CHORD?

MAJOR CHORDS have 4 half steps between the root and the third.

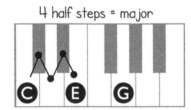

WHAT IS A MINOR CHORD?

MINOR CHORDS have 3 half steps between the root and the third.

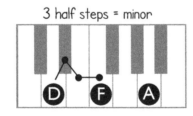

HOW TO MAKE A MAJOR CHORD MINOR

To make a major chord minor, LOWER the third a half step.

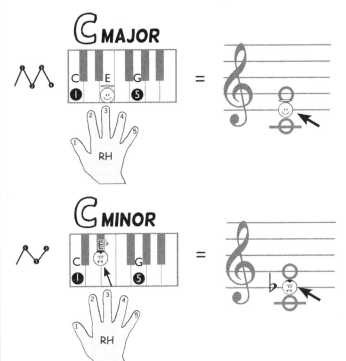

HOW TO MAKE A MINOR CHORD MAJOR

To make a minor chord major, RAISE the third a half step.

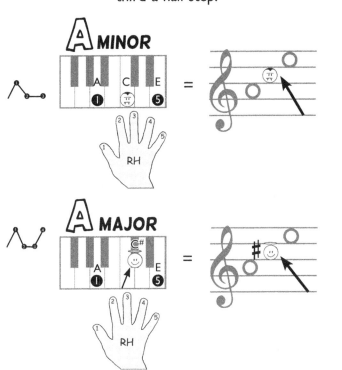

5. MAJOR TO MINOR

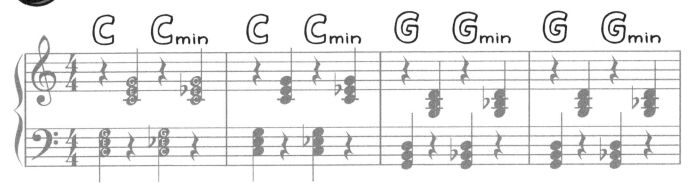

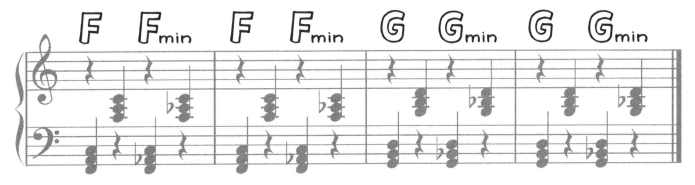

Review

REVIEW: ROOT NOTES AND CHORD SYMBOLS

 ## CHORD SYMBOL CRASH LANDING

Take note of the chord symbols below. Which chords are minor?

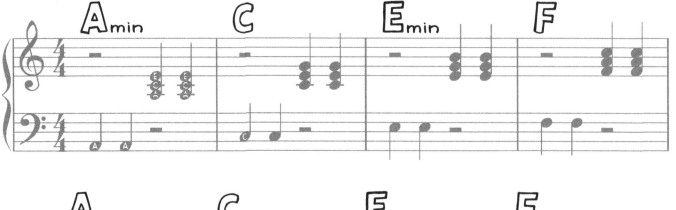

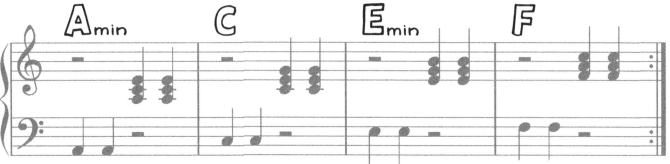

REVIEW: CHORD PROGRESSIONS

 ## MODAL METEOR PROGRESSION REVIEW

Play this exercise and see if you can identify the chord progression.
(Hint: look at the chord symbols!)

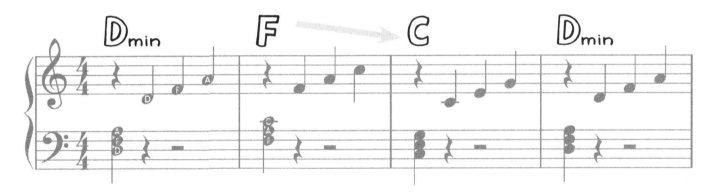

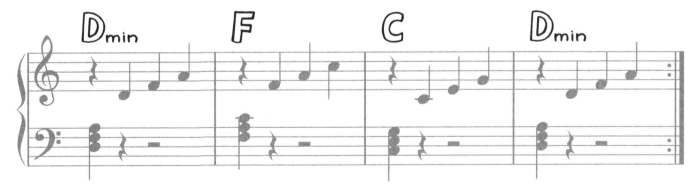

CHORD PROGRESSION:

   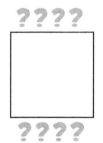

Review

QUANTUM QUIZ!

PATTERN 1: RH CHORD

PATTERN 2: LH ARPEGGIO

PATTERN 3: CREATE YOUR OWN

Try playing the patterns above starting on the different root notes below. Once you've mastered that, break free and explore by playing all over!

G A C E
F G D
C
A CHOOSE A ROOT NOTE!

MORE WAYS TO PLAY!

- Close your eyes. Point to any root note and play the pattern starting on that note.
- Use dice and roll to see which root note to use.
- Bonus: Try building both the major AND minor chords/arpeggios on these root notes!

COMMAND CENTER

Pattern Powers

- HANDS TOGETHER 🔒
- TRANSPOSITION 🔒
- OOM-PAH 🔒
- PULSE 🔒
- LEAD SHEETS 🔒
- ALBERTI 🔒
- POWER PROGRESSION 🔒

Creative Powers

- REVIEW ✓
- CREATIVITY 🔒
- EXPERIMENT 🔒
- KNOWLEDGE 🔒
- LISTENING 🔒
- ARTISTRY 🔒
- RHYTHM 🔒
- FEEL 🔒
- EXPLORE 🔒
- SONGWRITING 🔒
- VARIATION 🔒
- PERFORMANCE 🔒
- EXPRESSION 🔒

"Congrats! You've earned the 'Review' power!"

"Reviewing is a power?"

"Yes! Reviewing and reflecting are big parts of learning. Let's learn more!"

CHAPTER 2

ASTRO ARPEGGIOS

You already know that chords and arpeggios are the most powerful patterns in the musical universe. You also know that they are found in almost every song — from classical to rock... and beyond!

Now that you have mastered the basics, your journey is going to get interesting. You are going to be playing more complex patterns with both hands, up and down the scale. You will also be using these patterns with chord progressions to play whole songs.

Let's unlock the secrets of harmonic power!

Keep an eye out for crystals! When you find one, color it in. They can often be found where creativity is plentiful. You'll need them later!

Astro Arpeggios

8 DOUBLE STAR ARPEGGIO SCALE

A "TAIL" OF TWO COMETS

10 A SECTION: DOUBLE ARPEGGIO

Arpeggios, hands together.

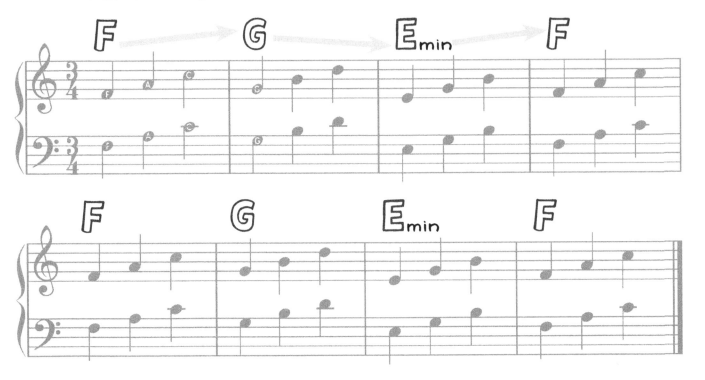

Astro Arpeggios

11. B SECTION: ARPEGGIO, CHORD

Left hand plays an arpeggio while your right hand plays a chord.

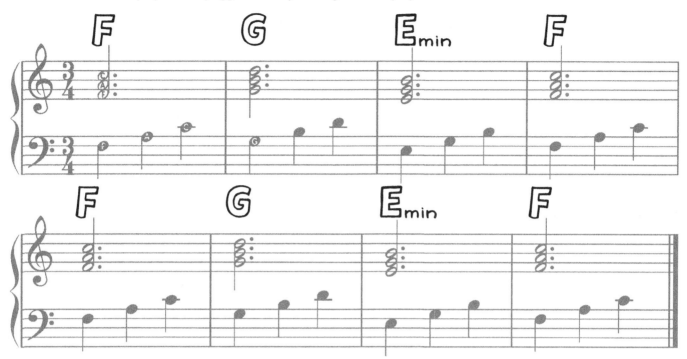

12. C SECTION: CHORD, ARPEGGIO

Left hand play a chord while your right hand plays an arpeggio.

Put the sections together. The song form is A B C A. What other form can you make? Show me you have mastered this by creating your own.

Astro Arpeggios

ARPEGGIO MACHINE

PLAY THE PATTERN...

LEFT HAND RIGHT HAND

Be sure to play both hands together on beat one.

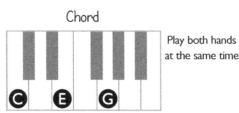

Chord

Play both hands at the same time

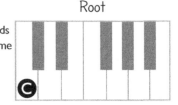

Root

- Start with both hands in C position.
- With your LH, play a chord, and at the SAME TIME play a C note with your RH.
- While still holding down the LH chord, play an E with your RH.
- While still holding down the LH chord, play a G with your RH.
- While still holding down the LH chord, play another E with your RH.
- Practice until smooth.

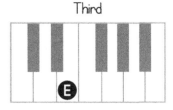

Third

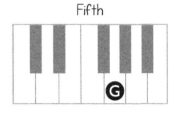

Fifth

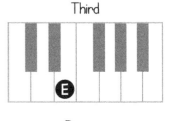

Third

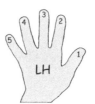

Root
Third
Fifth
Third

Astro Arpeggios

13 ROCK THE SCALE

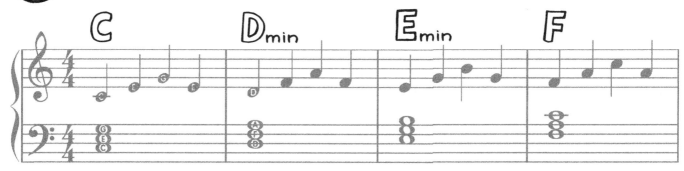

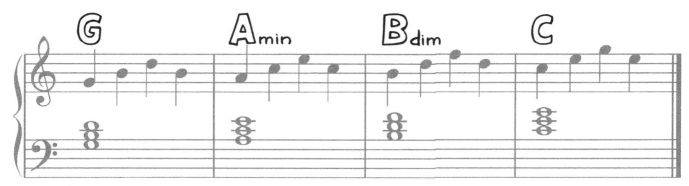

14 SCALE THE ROCK

Now LH takes the arpeggio pattern. Play your way back down the scale.

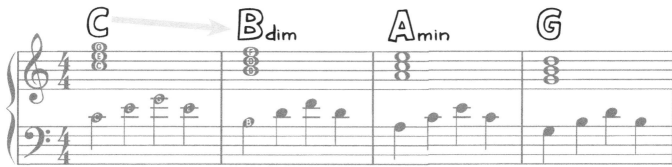

Try these exercises with a metronome!

Astro Arpeggios

BLACK HOLE BALLAD

15 A SECTION
Both hands play a root-third-fifth-third arpeggio pattern.

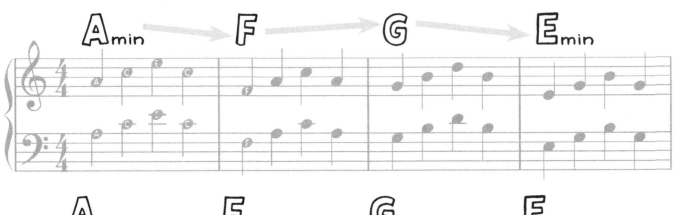

16 B SECTION
Left hand plays a chord while the right hand plays a root-third-fifth-third arpeggio pattern.

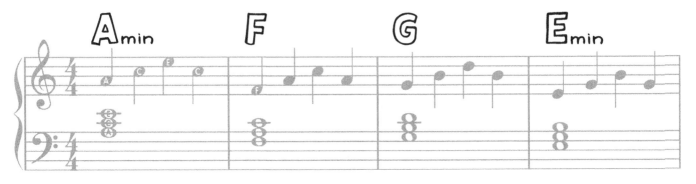

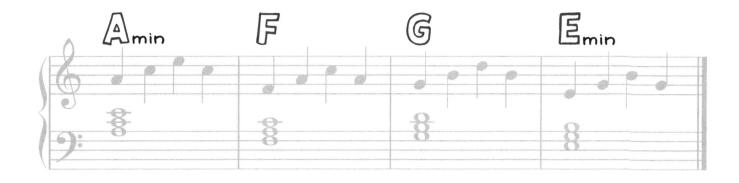

17) C SECTION

Right hand plays a chord while the left hand plays a root-third-fifth-third arpeggio pattern.

Astro Arpeggios

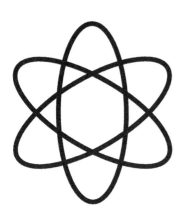

LET'S EXPERIMENT!

For this activity, combine chords to build your own progressions! Then combine them with patterns from this chapter for amazing results!

STEP 1 CHOOSE FROM THESE CHORDS

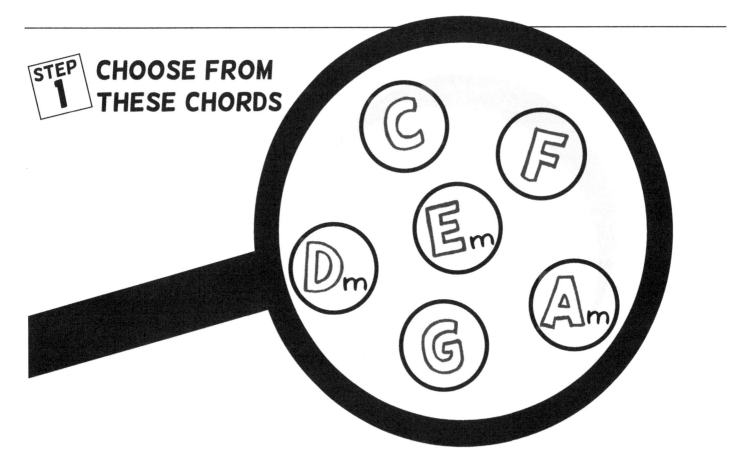

STEP 2 BUILD A PROGRESSION BY COMBINING 4 CHORDS FROM ABOVE LIKE OUR EXAMPLE:

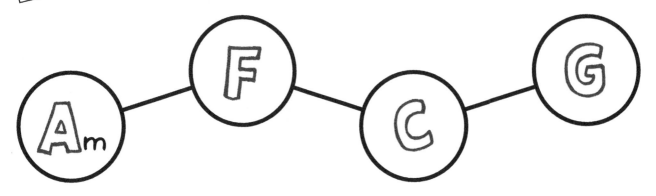

STEP 3: SEE YOUR RESULTS!

Play and experiment until you find progressions you like!

EXPERIMENT

PROGRESSION 1:
Play this progression with a LH Chord/RH arpeggio pattern.
(Like "Cosmic Combo" on page 13.)

Notes: (lyrics, dynamics, etc.)
_____
_____
_____

PROGRESSION 2:
Play this progression with a bottom-middle-top-middle arpeggio progression like in "Black Hole Ballad" on page 18.

Notes: _____
_____

PROGRESSION 3:
Choose your own rhythm pattern!

Notes: _____
_____
_____

Tip! Progressions don't always have to contain 4 chords. It's common to have progressions with 8 or 12 chords, too. See if you can come up with a longer progression!

Astro Arpeggios

QUANTUM QUIZ!

1. KNOWLEDGE:
WHAT DOES "SONG FORM" MEAN?

_____

_____

2. PLAY
PLAY ARPEGGIOS, HANDS TOGETHER, STARTING ON THESE ROOT NOTES:

- C — COMPLETE! ☐
- G — COMPLETE! ☐
- Dm — COMPLETE! ☐
- F — COMPLETE! ☐

3. PERFORM
PERFORM ONE OF YOUR PROGRESSIONS FROM THE "EXPERIMENT" PAGE FOR FRIENDS OR FAMILY. ADD CREATIVITY, LIKE LYRICS OR ARTWORK!

COMPLETE! ☐

"Congratulations! You've earned these powers."

"Let's move things around!"

"Transposition, here we come!"

COMMAND CENTER

Pattern Powers
- HANDS TOGETHER
- TRANSPOSITION 🔒
- OOM-PAH 🔒
- PULSE 🔒
- LEAD SHEETS 🔒
- ALBERTI 🔒
- POWER PROGRESSION 🔒

Creative Powers
- REVIEW ✓
- CREATIVITY
- EXPERIMENT
- KNOWLEDGE 🔒
- LISTENING 🔒
- ARTISTRY 🔒
- RHYTHM 🔒
- FEEL 🔒
- EXPLORE 🔒
- SONGWRITING 🔒
- VARIATION 🔒
- PERFORMANCE 🔒
- EXPRESSION 🔒

Astro Arpeggios

CHAPTER 3
TRANSPOSITION

CHORD COMPLAINT DEPARTMENT

You may have noticed that the songs in Chord Quest (with just a couple of exceptions) use exclusively white keys in the key of C. We've done that on purpose because, with no sharps or flats, C is an easy key to learn in. There are actually many other keys, though! You can move chords, patterns and melodies to any key using something called transposition. Let's check it out!

TOP REASONS TO TRANSPOSE

MISSION: TRANSPOSITION

TACKLING TRANSPOSITION

HOW TRANSPOSITION WORKS

Each major key maintains the same relationships between notes and chords, even though it starts in a different place. Some keys have sharps and flats, which are needed to maintain those relationships. Because of them, we can move from key to key without changing the character of the song. It will just sound higher or lower.

WANT PROOF? PLAY A C SCALE:

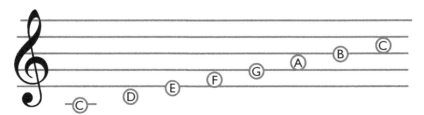

NOW PLAY A G SCALE:

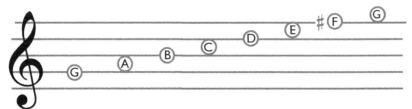

HOW DO I FIGURE OUT WHAT "KEY" A SONG IS IN?

1) Look at the key signature (the key signature is a group of 1 or more sharps or flats right after the clef). If there are sharps and flats at the beginning before the time signature, you can use them to figure out the key. Having NO sharps or flats at the beginning generally means you're in the key of C (or possibly A minor). Look at the chord scale glossary on page 82 to see the key signatures for different keys.)

2) Find "home base." Is there a chord that feels like "home base"? If so, the name of that chord is also probably the name of the key. Songs often end on that "home base" chord, like the song on page 28. It ends on C and has no sharps or flats. It's in the key of C.

3) Ask for help. Still not sure? Ask a music teacher, or search online - there are tools and sites that can help you figure out the key.

LET'S LOOK AT CHORD SCALES

"This is the C chord scale. You're quite familiar with these chords by now."

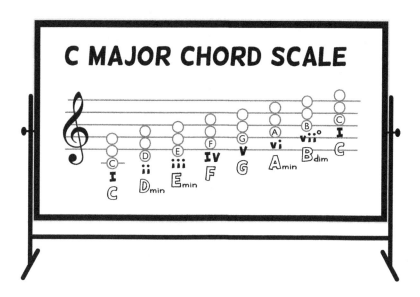

"This is the G chord scale. Notice that the chord numbers stay the same. That's because the relationships are the same."

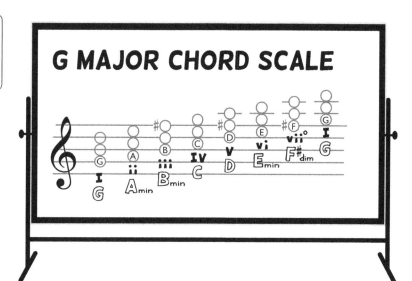

PLAY BOTH CHORD SCALES ABOVE. SEE HOW THEY SOUND SIMILAR?

- [ ] **COMPLETE!** Play the C major chord scale
- [ ] **COMPLETE!** Play the G major chord scale
- [ ] **COMPLETE!** Reflect: do they sound alike?

You can use scales and chord scales to help you transpose. On the next page, we'll show you the steps to transpose your favorite songs!

Transposition

TRANSPOSING IN 4 STEPS

Let's transpose this simple song:

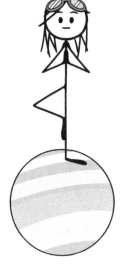

Are there any sharps or flats in the key signature? What feels like "home base"? (See page 26 for more tips on finding the key.)

The song ends on C and we have no sharps or flats. **We're in the key of C.**

The pattern is:

RH: Chord
LH: Root Note

Compare the chord progression above to the C chord scale. If we do that, we'll see that the progression is:

I   ii   IV   V   I

Referring to the chord progression by its chord numbers makes it easy to change keys.

Use the chord numbers to figure out what the chord progression is in the new key. Let's transpose to the key of G.

In the key of G:

I   ii   IV   V   I   =   G   Am   C   D   G

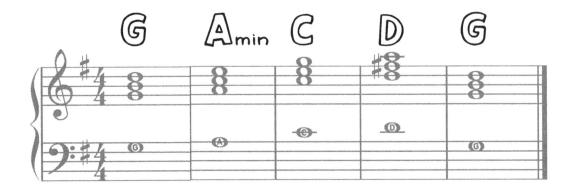

28

Transposition

PRACTICE TRANSPOSING

Now, practice your new skill by transposing the song below to the key of D! Follow the steps and fill them in as you go! Turn to the Chord Scale Glossary on page 82 to view the chord scale for the key of D.

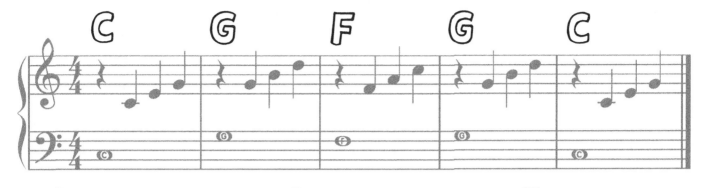

FIGURE OUT THE KEY 1

The song above is in the key of:

FIGURE OUT THE PATTERNS 2

RH: _____

LH: _____

FIGURE OUT THE PROGRESSION 3

The progression (using chord numbers/Roman numerals):

___ ___ ___ ___ ___

TRANSPOSE AND PLAY 4

In the key of D:

___ ___ ___ ___ ___ = ___ ___ ___ ___ ___

Chord numbers from above   Chord symbols (letters) for the key of D

For an answer key to this activity (and much more!) visit mwfunstuff.com/cq2

Transposition

TRANSPOSING PACHELBEL

Let's play Pachelbel in C major, and then transpose it to D major - Pachelbel's original key!

18 PACHELBEL'S CANON IN C

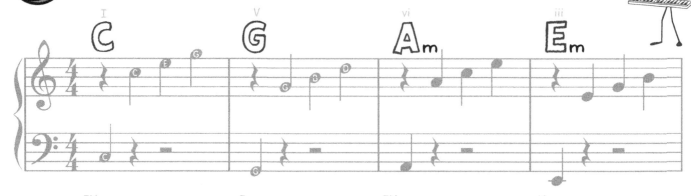

19 PACHELBEL'S CANON IN C, STYLE 2

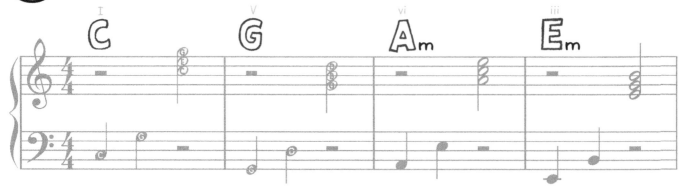
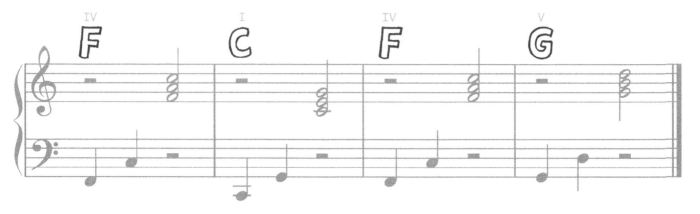

20 PACHELBEL'S CANON IN D

Write in the chord symbols! If you need to see the chord scale for D major, turn to page 82.

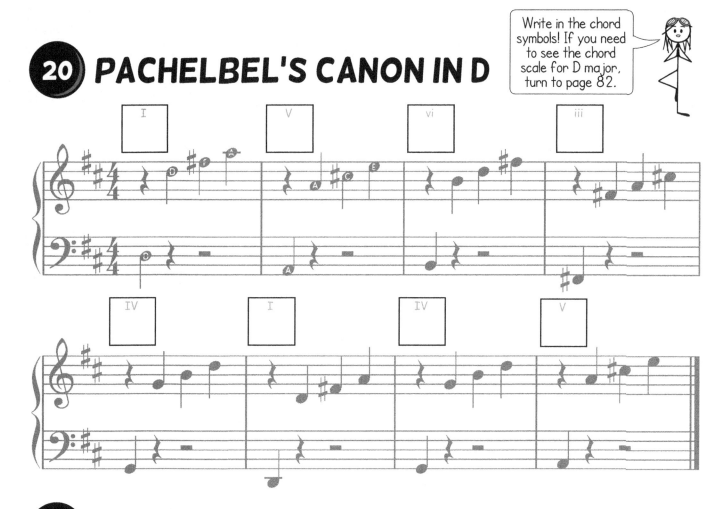

21 PACHELBEL'S CANON IN D, STYLE 2

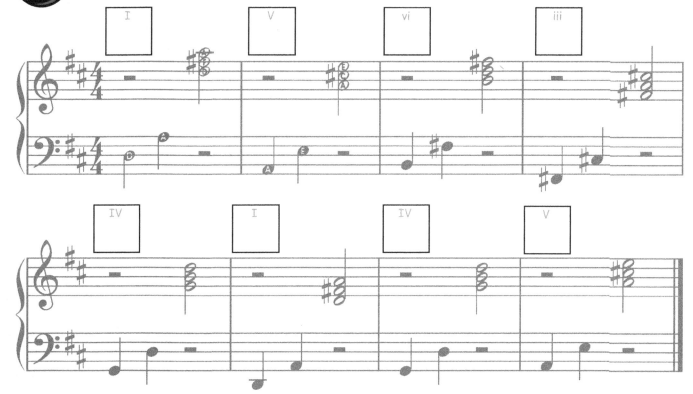

For an answer key to this activity (and much more!) visit mwfunstuff.com/cq2

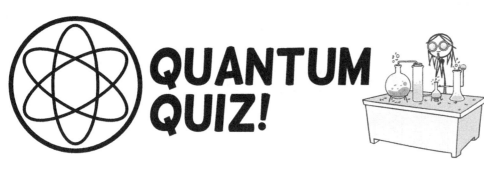

QUANTUM QUIZ!

1. KNOWLEDGE
TO TRANSPOSE SOMETHING, WE MOVE IT TO ANOTHER _____.

2. KNOWLEDGE:
HOW MANY SHARPS ARE IN THE KEY OF G? USE THE CHART ON PAGE 82 TO FIND THE ANSWER.

_____

3. TRANSPOSE
PERFORM THE SONG FROM PAGE 28 IN BOTH ITS KEYS. SING SOME "LA LA LAS" OR "OOHS." WHICH KEY IS PERSONALLY BETTER FOR YOUR VOICE?

COMPLETE! ☐

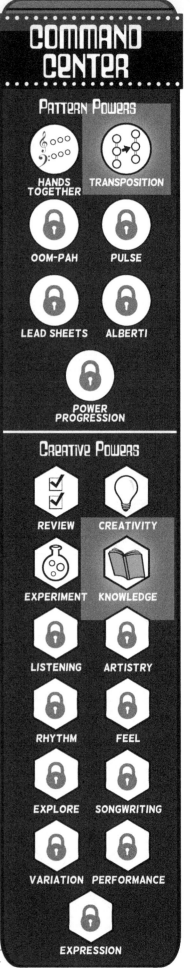

Transposition

CHAPTER 4
OOM-PAH

Many of us think of Oom-pah music and respond with a smile — imagining polka bands, circus music or, of course, the Oompa Loompas from Willy Wonka's Chocolate Factory.

But the Oom-pah pattern is full of even more surprises. It is a true power pattern used in a wide variety of styles and has a rich history. Eastern European classical composers like Strauss, Brahms and Chopin all used Oom-pah patterns in their waltzes. A popular style of Klezmer music (a traditional Jewish style) came out of this same part of the world, and also shows an Oom-pah influence.

The Oom-pah list goes on and on. Ragtime players used it. Even famous composer Danny Elfman (who has written the soundtracks for TONS of movies... including the Simpsons' theme song!) uses Oom-pah... and so can you!

OOM-PAH-PAH WALTZES

The "oom" is the low note (the root note) on the down beat, kind of like the boom of a drum.

The "pahs" are the higher notes of the chord.

LEFT HAND

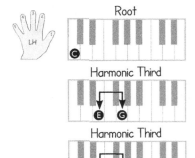

RIGHT HAND

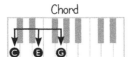

- Left hand plays the root, followed by a harmonic third (with the 1 and 3 fingers), and another harmonic third.

- Practice that until smooth, and then try adding your right hand, playing a chord while the left hand plays the root note.

Together, left, left! Tap it on your legs first.

22) CELESTIAL CIRCUS

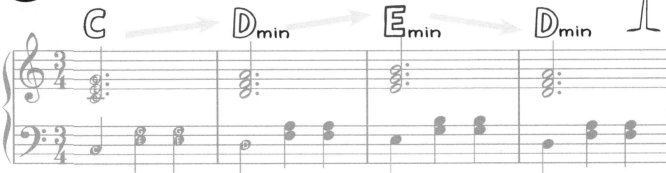

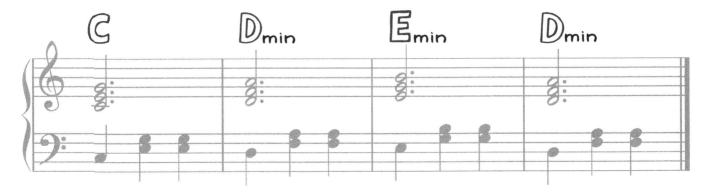

23 WALTZ OF WHIMSY

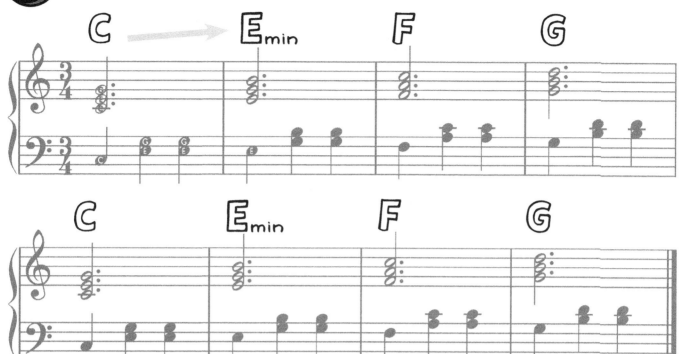

24 TRANSPOSITION TRAPEZE

Now that you've mastered the pattern, let's fly on over to a new key. In this exercise, we'll be transposing exercise #22, "Celestial Circus," to the key of G. Write the new chord symbols above each measure, and then play.

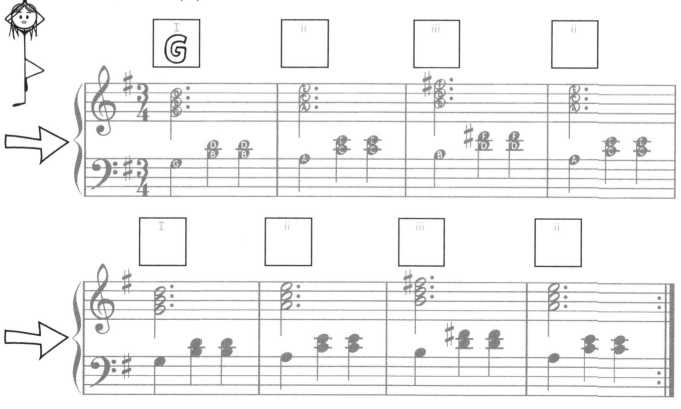

Oom-Pah

OOM-PAH OOM-PAH

LEFT HAND

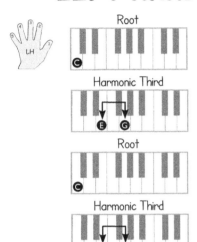

RIGHT HAND

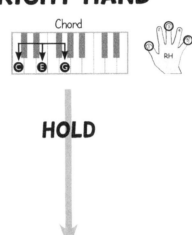

HOLD

- Left hand plays the root, followed by a harmonic third (with the 1 and 3 fingers), then root and harmonic third again.
- Practice that until smooth, and then try adding your right hand, playing a chord when the left hand plays the root note and holding for four beats.

25 OOM-PAH OOM-PAH

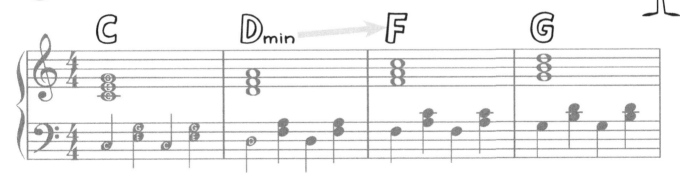

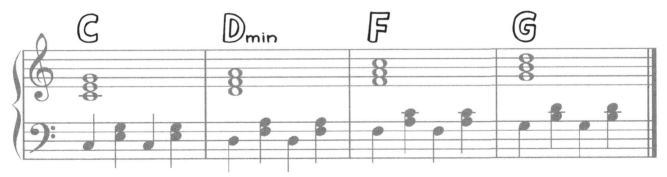

OOM-PAH DOO WOP

LEFT HAND RIGHT HAND

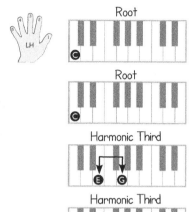
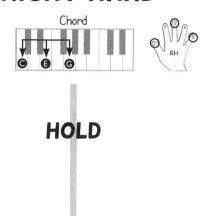

- Left hand plays the root note and then another root note.
- Next, it "bounces" to a harmonic third (with the 1 and 3 fingers) and repeats that harmonic third.
- Practice that until smooth, and then try adding your right hand, playing a chord when the left hand plays the root note and holding for four beats.

You can play this exercise as the accompaniment to the famous "Heart and Soul" duet.

26 OOM-PAH DOO WOP

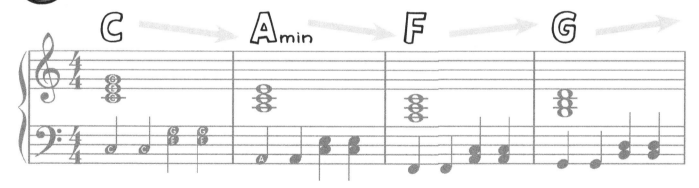

Oom-Pah

KLEZMERIZED

LEFT HAND RIGHT HAND

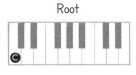
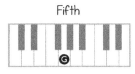
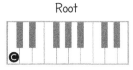
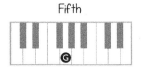

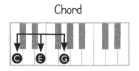
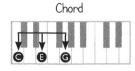
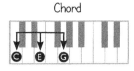
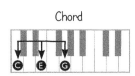

- On beat one, the left hand plays the root note.
- On beat two, the right hand plays the chord.
- On beat three, the left hand plays the <u>fifth</u>.
- On beat four, the right hand plays the chord again.
- Repeat the pattern.

PRACTICE IN C POSITION UNTIL SMOOTH

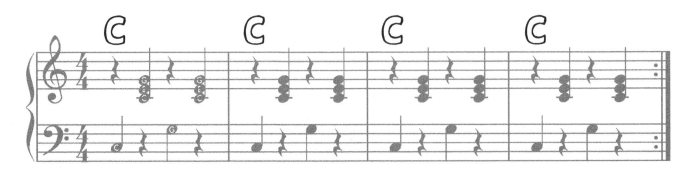

Oom-Pah

27 KLEZMERIZED

Play the E major chord instead of E minor. Just play a G# instead of G every time. It's been Klezmerized!

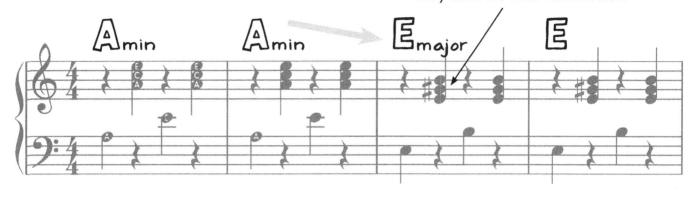
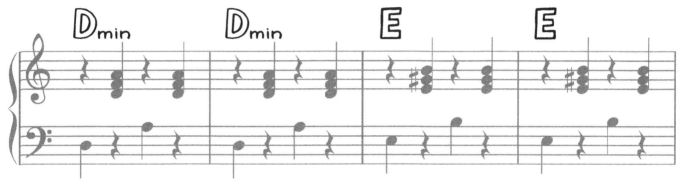
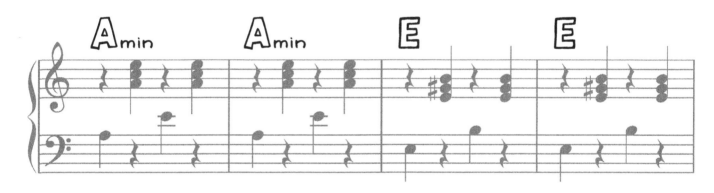
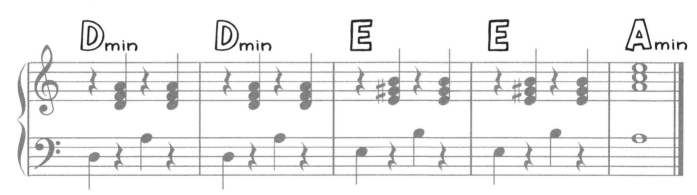

Look at and listen to Klezmer music online.

LISTENING

Oom-Pah

OOM-PAH BAND, KLEZMER STYLE

This is a variation of the classic "Malaguena" progression.

28 ANDALUSIAN ARPEGGIOS

Left hand plays the root-third-fifth-third pattern while the right hand plays a chord.

29 ANDALUSIAN OOM-PAH

Left hand plays root-harmonic third, root-harmonic third while the right hand plays a chord.

30. ANDALUSIAN ROOT FIFTH PATTERN

Left hand plays the root, right hand plays a chord, left hand plays the fifth and then right hand plays a chord again.

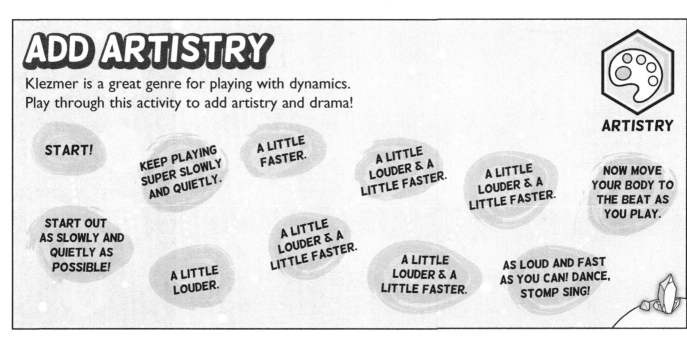

ADD ARTISTRY

Klezmer is a great genre for playing with dynamics. Play through this activity to add artistry and drama!

ARTISTRY

- START!
- START OUT AS SLOWLY AND QUIETLY AS POSSIBLE!
- KEEP PLAYING SUPER SLOWLY AND QUIETLY.
- A LITTLE LOUDER.
- A LITTLE FASTER.
- A LITTLE LOUDER & A LITTLE FASTER.
- A LITTLE LOUDER & A LITTLE FASTER.
- A LITTLE LOUDER & A LITTLE FASTER.
- A LITTLE LOUDER & A LITTLE FASTER.
- NOW MOVE YOUR BODY TO THE BEAT AS YOU PLAY.
- AS LOUD AND FAST AS YOU CAN! DANCE, STOMP SING!

Oom-Pah

QUANTUM QUIZ!

PLAY THESE PROGRESSIONS WITH YOUR FAVORITE OOM-PAH PATTERNS:

- C A$_{min}$ G F
- D$_{min}$ E$_{min}$ F G
- A$_{min}$ F G E$_{maj}$
- CREATE YOUR OWN!

COMPLETE! ☐ (×4)

COMMAND CENTER

Pattern Powers
- HANDS TOGETHER
- TRANSPOSITION
- OOM-PAH
- PULSE 🔒
- LEAD SHEETS 🔒
- ALBERTI 🔒
- POWER PROGRESSION 🔒

Creative Powers
- REVIEW
- CREATIVITY
- EXPERIMENT
- KNOWLEDGE
- LISTENING
- ARTISTRY
- RHYTHM 🔒
- FEEL 🔒
- EXPLORE 🔒
- SONGWRITING 🔒
- VARIATION 🔒
- PERFORMANCE 🔒
- EXPRESSION 🔒

Congratulations! You've earned Oom-pah, Artistry and Listening powers!

The patterns made it easy!

Let's learn patterns from rock music!

Oom-Pah

CHAPTER 5

RHYTHM RUMBLE

A piano + your imagination = a band at your fingertips.

Your left hand becomes the low notes, like a bass guitar...

And your right hand becomes the higher notes, like a guitar or voice.

Many famous rock stars write their new songs on the piano first...

Like the Beatles!

then assign parts to their band members.

Now channel your inner rock star as you make music that same way!

By the end of this book you will be aware of the musical power you have (if you haven't realized it already). Because you understand chord progressions and rhythmic patterns on the piano, you can compose for all types of instruments and groups — tubas and cellos or folk bands and orchestras. Or, as you will soon see, you can even create music for a ROCK BAND.

Let's see how the piano can rock!

Rock music? The only rocks in MY music books are BORING songs ABOUT rocks!

BRING IN THE BASS

LEFT HAND

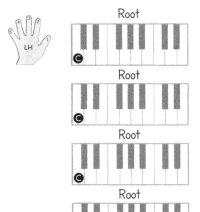

RIGHT HAND

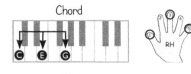

HOLD

- Left hand plays quarter note root notes.
- Right hand plays a chord for four beats.

31 FEEL THE BEAT

Left hand plays pulsing quarter notes while the right hand plays a chord.

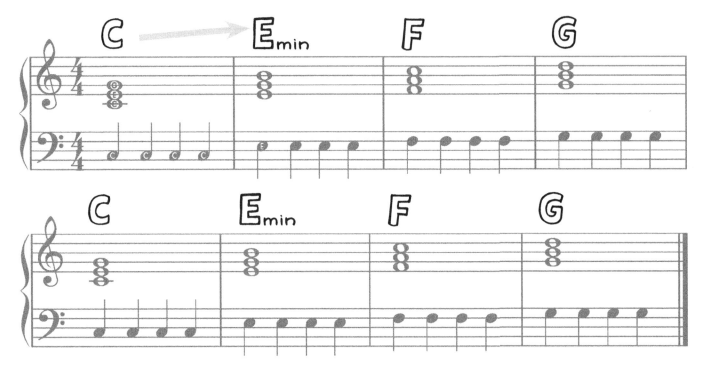

Rhythm Rumble

LEFT HAND

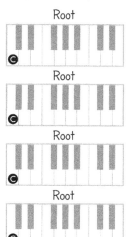

RIGHT HAND
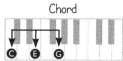

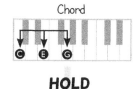

- Left hand plays quarter note root notes.
- Right hand plays chords on beats one and three, holding for two beats each.

32 DRIVE THE BEAT

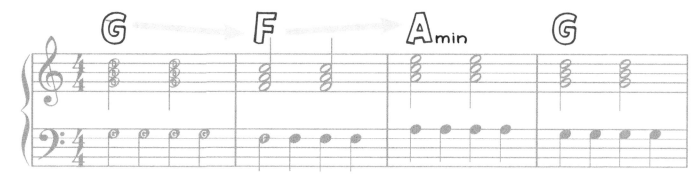

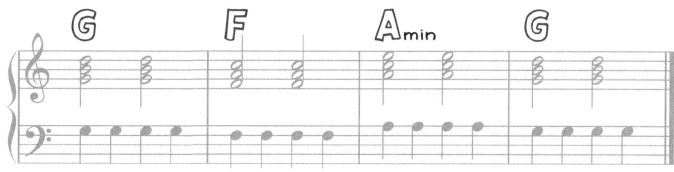

Rhythm Rumble

MOVE IT

LEFT HAND

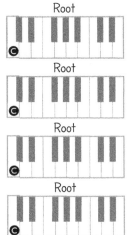

RIGHT HAND

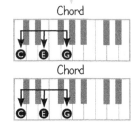

- Left hand plays quarter note root notes.
- Right hand plays a half note chord on beat one, and quarter note chords on beats three and four.

33 MOVE IT

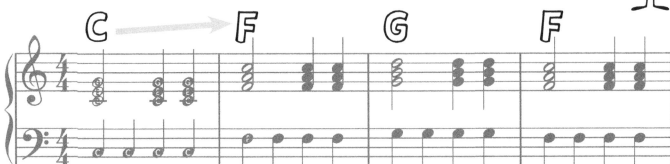

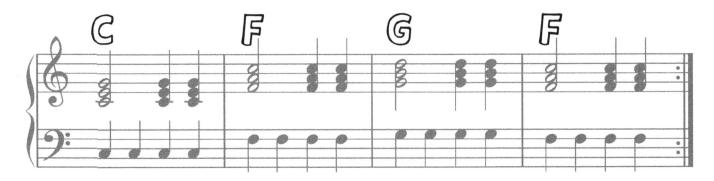

Rhythm Rumble

LEFT HAND

RIGHT HAND

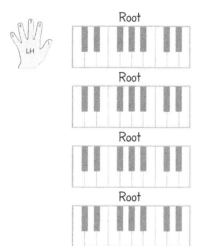
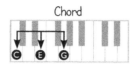

HOLD

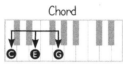

- Left hand plays quarter note root notes.
- Right hand plays a chord on beat one and holds for three beats, then plays another chord on beat four.

Together, left, left, together!

34 GROOVE IT

This reminds me of "Louie, Louie!"

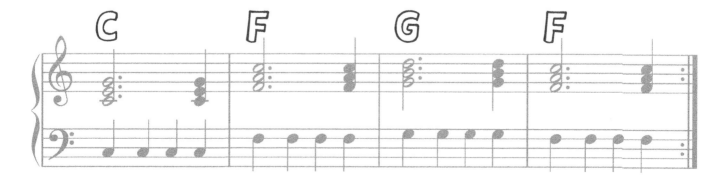

Rhythm Rumble

FACE THE FIFTHS

LEFT HAND   RIGHT HAND

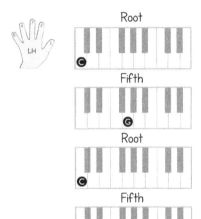
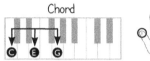

HOLD

- Left hand plays the root, then the fifth, then another root and another fifth.
- Right hand plays a chord on beat one and holds for four beats.

35 FACE THE FIFTHS

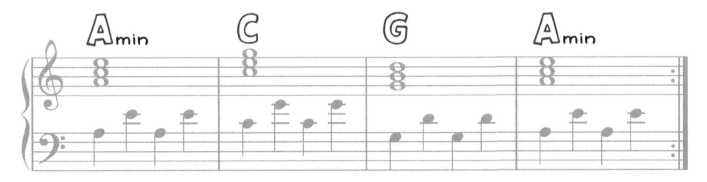

48 Rhythm Rumble

FIFTHS ROCK

LEFT HAND   RIGHT HAND

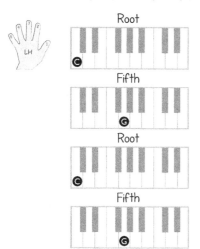
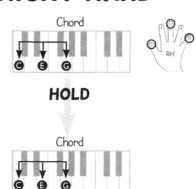

- Left hand plays the root, then the fifth, then another root and another fifth.
- Right hand plays a chord on beats one and three, holding for two beats each.

36 FIFTHS ROCK

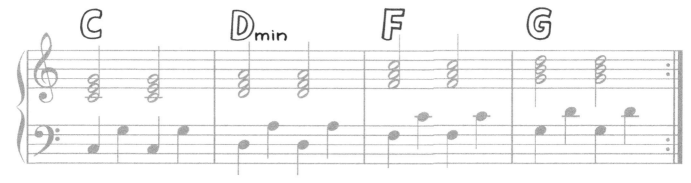

Rhythm Rumble

CHORD ROCK

LEFT HAND

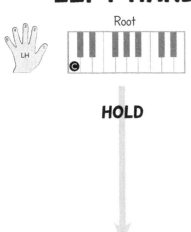

HOLD

RIGHT HAND

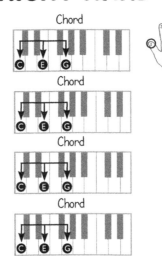

- Left hand plays the root and holds for four beats.
- Right hand plays a chord on beats one, two, three and four.

37 CHORD ROCK IN C MAJOR

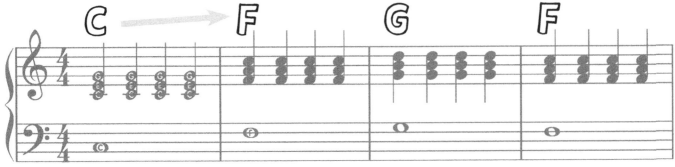

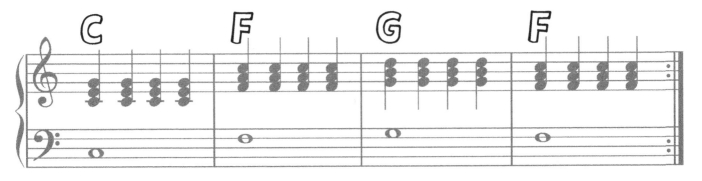

TRANSPOSE: CHORD ROCK IN G MAJOR

Exercise your transposition skills by transposing "Chord Rock" to the key of G. Write in the new chord symbols and play.

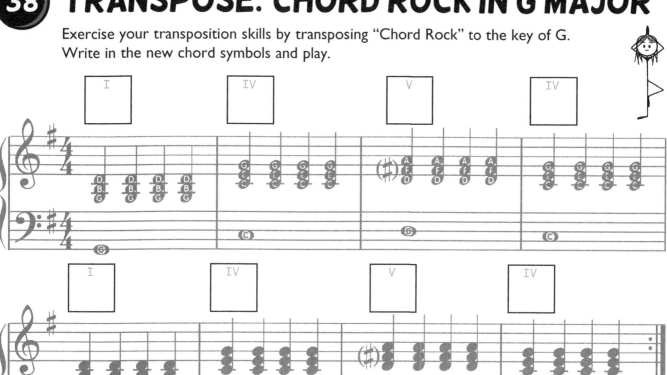

TRANSPOSE: CHORD ROCK IN D MAJOR

Now transpose Chord Rock to the key of D!

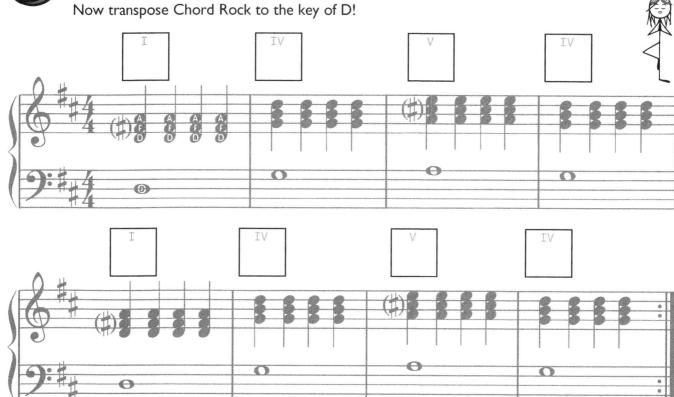

QUANTUM QUIZ!

COMBINE THE CHORD PROGRESSIONS FROM THE LEFT WITH THE RHYTHMS FROM THE RIGHT AND PLAY.

COMPLETE!

COMMAND CENTER

Pattern Powers

HANDS TOGETHER — TRANSPOSITION

OOM-PAH — PULSE

LEAD SHEETS — ALBERTI

POWER PROGRESSION

Creative Powers

REVIEW — CREATIVITY

EXPERIMENT — KNOWLEDGE

LISTENING — ARTISTRY

RHYTHM — FEEL

EXPLORE — SONGWRITING

VARIATION — PERFORMANCE

EXPRESSION

Look how much you've learned! By now, you can play chords and chord progressions, and come up with your own ideas using them. Here's another fun way you can use your chord knowledge: to play cover songs!

One of the rewards of knowing how to play chords is that it allows you to play your favorite songs by your favorite artists. When you play a song that was written and performed by someone else, it's called a "cover song." The chord progressions for many of these can be found online, or as part of printed sheet music. Now that you can identify chord symbols and play chords, all of these songs are open to you!

In this chapter, you'll learn how to apply the knowledge you already have to the songs you love. There's no limit to what you can do!

Super Skill: Lead Sheets

HOW DO YOU PLAY A LEAD SHEET?

 PRACTICE PLAYING JUST THE CHORDS WITH YOUR LEFT HAND:

This song just uses three chords: C, F and G.

 STEP 2: PRACTICE SINGING THE MELODY OR PLAYING THE MELODY WITH YOUR RH.

Super challenge: try singing and playing at the same time!

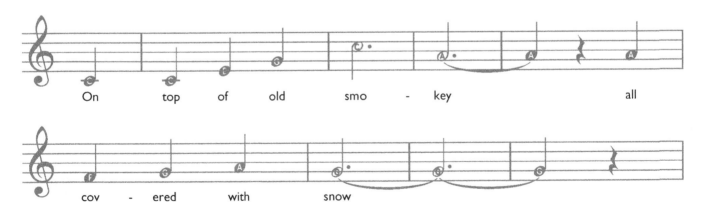

Super Skill: Lead Sheets

STEP 3: PUT IT TOGETHER!

With your left hand, play the chords at the place in the song where you would play the note or sing the word directly below it. If a measure doesn't have a new chord symbol written above it, you should keep playing the most recent chord. (I'll remind you at those spots to make it easier for now!) At the same time, sing the melody or play it with your right hand (or both!). Let's play!

Super Skill: Lead Sheets

COVER SONGS: ONLINE TOOLS

 SEARCH FOR THE SONG TITLE & THE WORD "CHORDS"

 **WHAT YOU WILL FIND WILL LOOK LIKE THIS:**

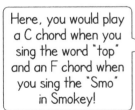

```
         C              F                         C
On top of Old Smokey, All covered with snow,
                        G                         C
I lost my true lover For courtin' too slow.
```

It's important to remember that you've learned the basic ingredients of a chord: the root, third (major or minor) and fifth. The chord progressions you find online may have some fancier chords, with extra ingredients (sevenths, diminished and augmented chords, etc.). Luckily, you should still be able to play most of your favorite songs, which won't have too many complicated chords. When you do encounter a "7" chord, you can omit the "7" (for now, that is – once you do learn seventh chords in Book 4, you'll be able to add them and appreciate the texture and color they bring to chords).

FOR EXAMPLE:

```
   C              F                    C
On top of Old Smokey, All covered with snow,
              G7                      C
I lost my true lover For courtin' too slow.
```

CAN BE PLAYED AS:

```
   C              F                    C
On top of Old Smokey, All covered with snow,
              G                       C
I lost my true lover For courtin' too slow.
```

Just make sure you pay attention to major and minor chords – which you should always play as written. Minor chords will be marked with a minus sign, the label "min," or an "m" like this:

```
C      G7         C
Home, home on the range
             Am        D7       G7
Where the deer and the antelope play
```

In this case, you can play the G7 chords as G chords, and the D7 chord as D. Just remember – that A should be minor, and that D should be major!

Super Skill: Lead Sheets

QUANTUM QUIZ!

1 KNOWLEDGE:
WHAT IS A "COVER SONG"?

_____

_____.

2 GOAL-SETTING:
MAKE A LIST OF AT LEAST TEN COVER SONGS YOU'D LIKE TO LEARN. REVISIT IT AND CHECK THEM OFF AS YOU COMPLETE THEM.

COVER SONG LIST:

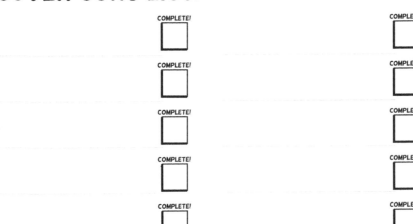

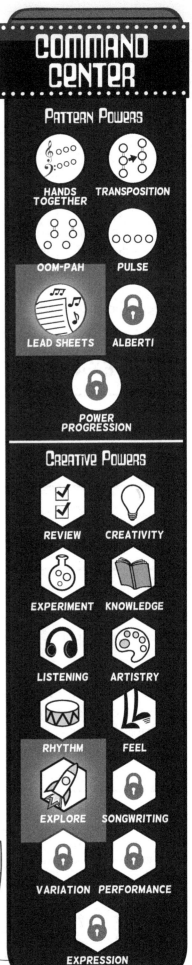

Super Skill: Lead Sheets

CHAPTER 7
ALBERTI BASS

Alberti bass is one of the most powerful and widely-used arpeggio patterns in the universe. The great masters of Vienna, Austria (Haydn, Mozart and Beethoven) immortalized Alberti bass by using the pattern in everything from keyboard and violin sonatas to compositions for their symphonies.

Mozart played and composed with the Alberti bass pattern... and now so can you!

DRATS! If people realize this simple pattern can have them playing and writing like Mozart, I'll go out of business!

HOW DO YOU PLAY ALBERTI BASS?

HOW DO YOU PLAY ALBERTI BASS?

You are an arpeggio expert, so it will be easy.

ALBERTI BASS IS: BOTTOM, TOP, MIDDLE, TOP

LEFT HAND ALBERTI BASS

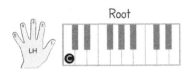
Root

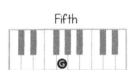
Fifth

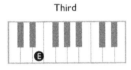
Third

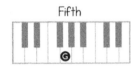
Fifth

RIGHT HAND

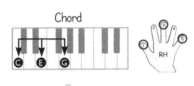
Chord

HOLD

- On beat one, the left hand plays the root note.
- On beat two, the left hand plays the fifth.
- On beat three, the left hand plays the third.
- On beat four, the left hand plays the fifth again. That's the Alberti bass pattern!
- Practice that until smooth, and then try adding your right hand. For this exercise, your right hand will play a chord on beat one and hold for four beats.

Bottom, top, middle, top.

PRACTICE IN C POSITION UNTIL SMOOTH

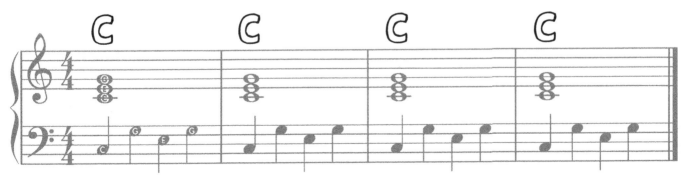

Alberti Bass

ALBERTI SCALE NUMBER 1

Go up the scale with your left hand playing the Alberti bass pattern and your right hand playing a chord.

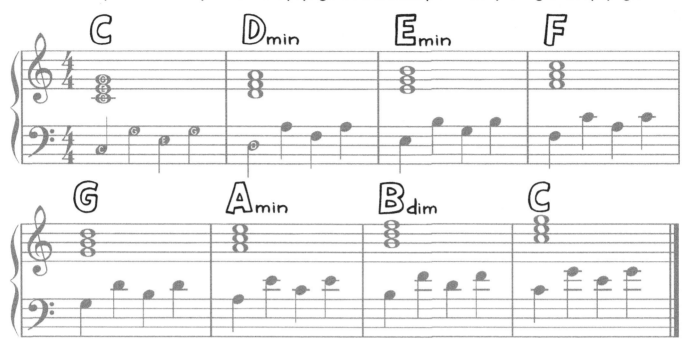

ALBERTI SCALE NUMBER 2

Now switch hands – play the Alberti pattern with your RH while playing a chord with your LH.

Try these exercises with a metronome!

DATE				RHYTHM CHALLENGE
SLOWEST				
FASTEST				

Alberti Bass

FULL MOON FANTASIA

42 A SECTION

Both hands play the Alberti pattern to this magical progression.

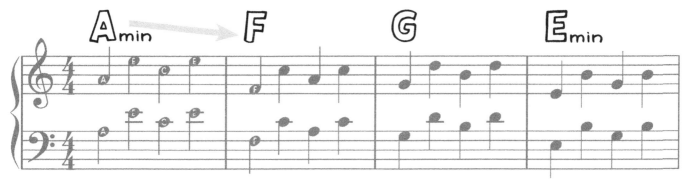

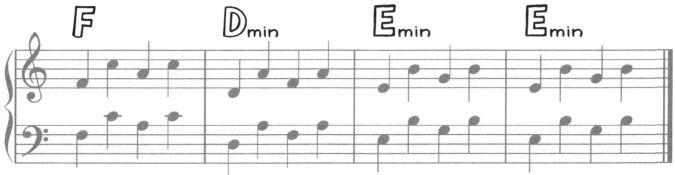

43 B SECTION

Left hand plays the Alberti bass pattern while your right hand plays a chord.

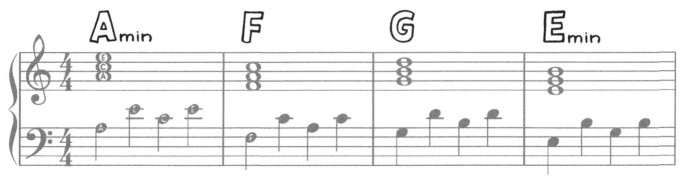

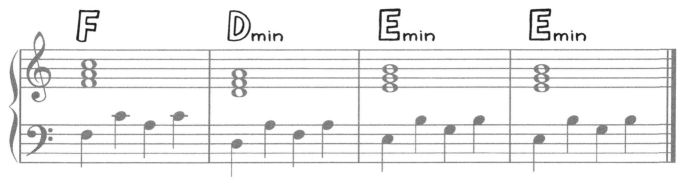

44 C SECTION

Right hand plays the Alberti pattern while your left hand plays a chord.

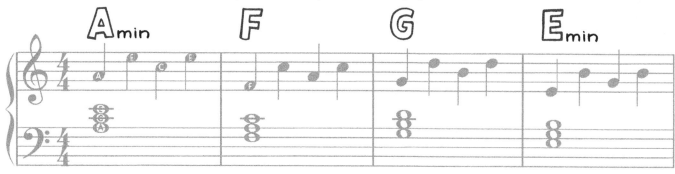

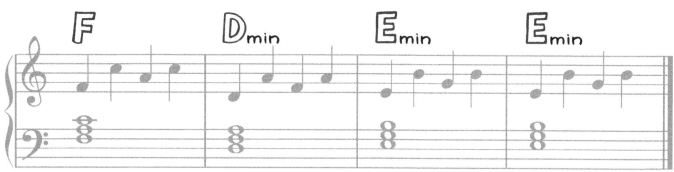

SONGWRITING
CREATE YOUR OWN SONG USING THE ALBERTI PATTERN!

SONG TITLE: _____

1 **WRITE A CHORD PROGRESSION:** ____ ____ ____ ____

2 **CHOOSE YOUR LH AND RH PATTERNS** (for example, LH Alberti, RH chord).

LH pattern: _____ RH pattern: _____

3 **ADD LYRICS, ADDITIONAL SECTIONS, AN ENDING, ETC.**
Note your additions/ideas here:

4 **ADD ARTISTRY, DYNAMICS, EFFECTS**
(pedal, loud, soft, etc.) and note them here:

SONGWRITING

Alberti Bass

PACHELBEL'S CANON

In these pieces, the most famous progression of all time (Pachelbel's Canon) meets one of the most famous classical patterns (Alberti bass).

45) VARIATION 1

Right hand plays the Alberti pattern while your left hand plays a chord. Note that the key is D major.

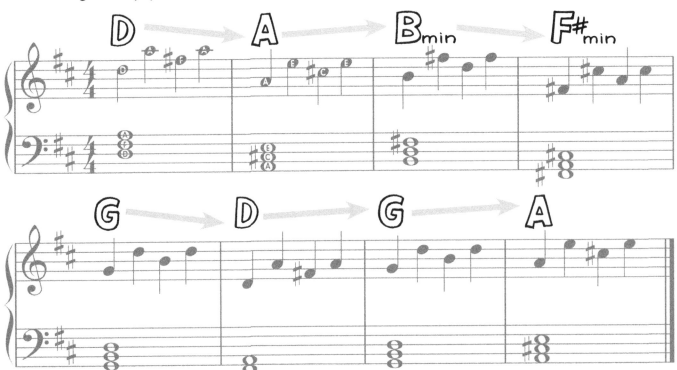

46) VARIATION 2

Left hand plays the Alberti pattern while your right hand plays a chord.

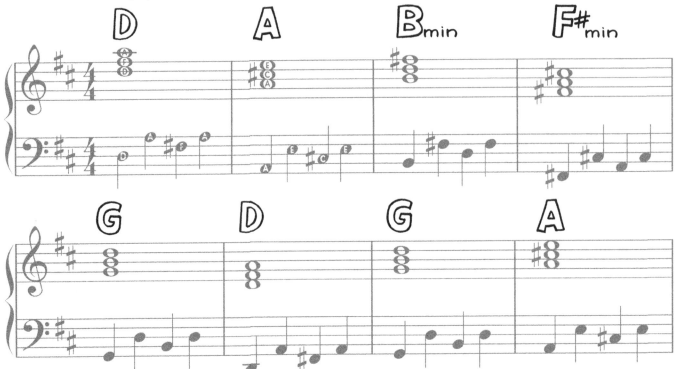

Alberti Bass

47 VARIATION 3

Left hand plays the Alberti pattern while your right hand plays a harmonic third.

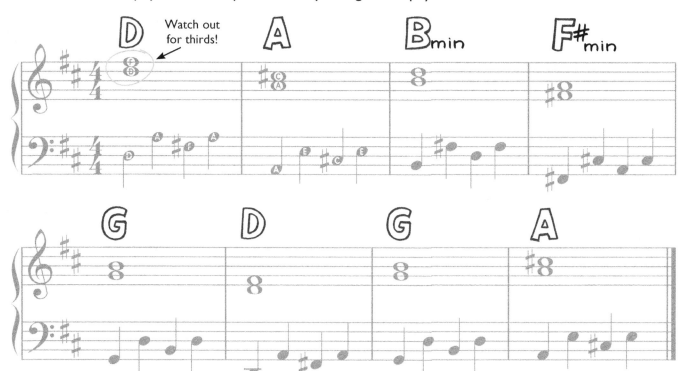

VARIATION

In music, you create a "variation" of a song by altering something, such as the melody, rhythm, harmony, arrangement, etc. Create your own variations of the Pachelbel progression by trying these changes:

RHYTHM: DOUBLE UP EACH NOTE OF THE ALBERTI PATTERN. BOTTOM-BOTTOM-TOP-TOP-MIDDLE-MIDDLE-TOP-TOP

HARMONY: CHANGE ONE CHORD OF THE PROGRESSION.

RHYTHM: HOLD THE FIRST NOTE OF THE ALBERTI PATTERN OUT LONGER. ONE TWO THREE AND FOUR AND.

MELODY: REMOVE ONE NOTE OF THE ALBERTI PATTERN TO CREATE A 3 NOTE PATTERN.

Alberti Bass

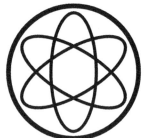

QUANTUM QUIZ!

1) KNOWLEDGE:
HOW DO YOU PLAY THE ALBERTI BASS PATTERN?

BOTTOM, _____ , _____ , _____ .

2) PLAY
PLAY THE PACHELBEL PROGRESSION FROM MEMORY, USING AN ALBERTI PATTERN.

COMPLETE! ☐

3) PERFORM
PERFORM THAT SAME PACHELBEL PATTERN FOR FAMILY OR FRIENDS.

COMPLETE! ☐

Tip - no one around? Record it and send it to someone to brighten their day!

Congratulations! You've earned Alberti, Songwriting and Variation Powers!

We can play like the masters!

I'm ready to learn something EPIC!

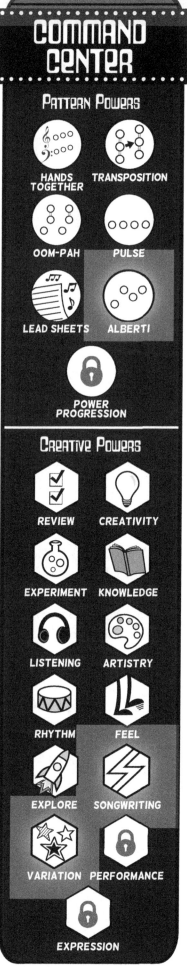

Alberti Bass

Here is a hit rock song secret (well, a secret that over 20 million people know): many hit songs were written with the same four chords. What are they? The chords are one, five, six and four - in the key of C, that's C, G, A minor and F.

You now have both the chops to perform like a rock star AND the secret of this powerful chord progression. The time has come for you to perform a concert medley of mega-platinum hits to a sold out audience.

For extra credit, be sure to sing some words. For triple credit, create your own epic rock song!

Universal Chord Concert

FOUR CHORD CONCERT

Hit list of I V vi IV songs

- Can You Feel the Love Tonight?
- Don't Stop Believing
- Bad Blood
- Wagon Wheel
- Demons
- The Scientist
- Hey Soul Sister
- With or Without You
- Love Story
- Halo
- I'm Yours
- Someone Like You
- Paparazzi

And MANY MORE!

48 MELODIC FIFTHS

Play these different patterns over the same epic progression (C, G, Amin, F).

Universal Chord Concert

49. BOTTOM MIDDLE TOP MIDDLE

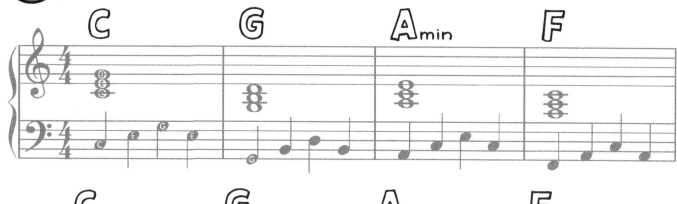

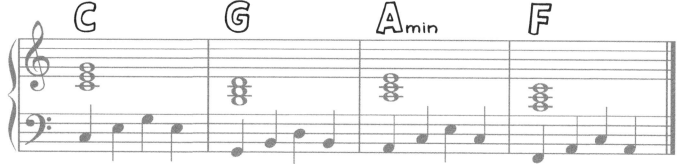

50. HALF NOTE CHORDS

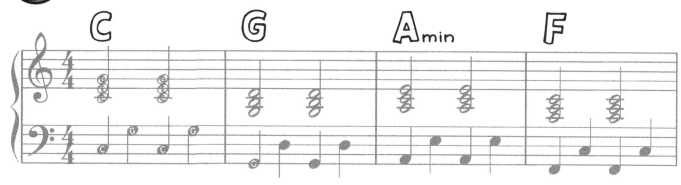

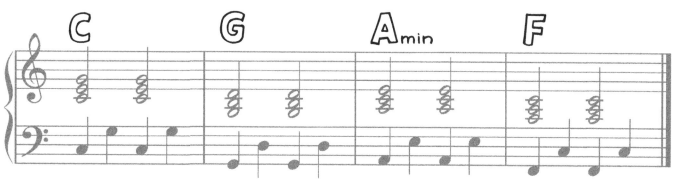

Universal Chord Concert

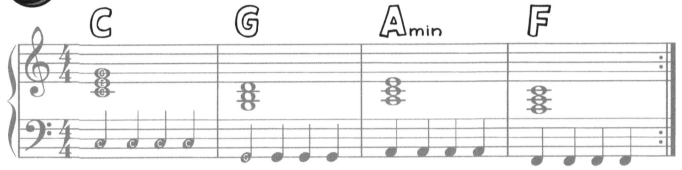

53 PULSE 3

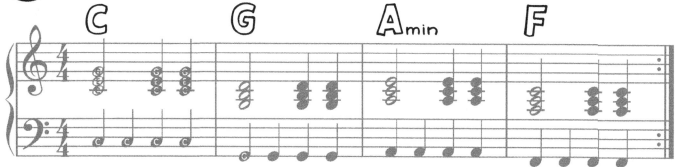

54 PULSE 4

55 MELODIC AND HARMONIC FIFTHS

Universal Chord Concert

BEST SET LIST IN THE UNIVERSE!

Prepare a list of songs for your concert with the I V vi IV Progression:

  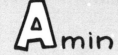

PERFORMANCE

Choose from the patterns you played in this chapter:

MELODIC FIFTHS

BOTTOM MIDDLE TOP MIDDLE

RH CHORDS, LH FIFTHS

RH WHOLE NOTE WITH LH PULSE

RH HALF NOTES WITH LH PULSE

RH HALF AND QUARTERS WITH LH PULSE

RH DOTTED HALF/ QUARTER WITH LH PULSE

MELODIC AND HARMONIC FIFTHS

☆ MY SET LIST ☆

EXAMPLE:

#48. Melodic Fifths

1.
2.
3.
4.
5.
6.
7.
8.

CREATE YOUR OWN LYRICS

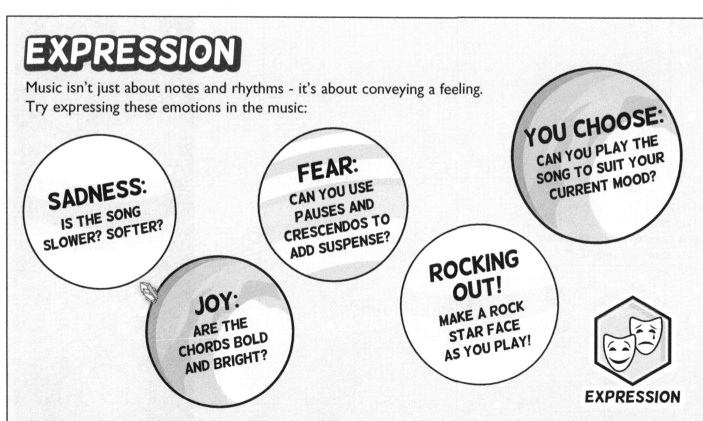

Universal Chord Concert

QUANTUM QUIZ!

1) PLAY!
PLAY THE "ONE FIVE SIX FOUR" PROGRESSION FROM MEMORY TWO DIFFERENT WAYS.

COMPLETE! ☐

2) PREPARE
YOUR CHORD QUEST TEST IS NEXT! ARE YOU READY? LIST ANY AREAS THAT MIGHT NEED REVIEW HERE, AND THEN GO BACK AND REFRESH.

"Congrats! You've earned your final powers for this book! It's time to return to headquarters and take your test!"

"AND DEFEAT THE BARON VON BORING!"

Universal Chord Concert

CHAPTER 9

You've come so far in this book – mastering powerful patterns and even performing your own epic four chord concert!

Still, there are two major accomplishments you have left to achieve — passing your Chord Quest Test AND defeating the Baron von Boring! If you can accomplish these things, you'll be free to portal ahead to Chord Quest Powerful Piano Lessons Level 3.

Like in the last book, you'll be using the skills you've learned to create music and then recording and sharing your creativity with the universe. If you don't feel ready, you may want to go back and review first.

If you're up for the challenge, turn the page. Good luck!

CHORD QUEST TEST

You've completed your training in Meridee Winters Chord Quest Powerful Piano Lessons Level 2, and are now ready for your Chord Quest test. If you can defeat the Baron von Boring, your quest will be complete and you can portal to Level 3! Are you ready?

1. REFLECT AND PREPARE:

COMPLETE! ☐

1. Reflect on all the skills you've gained during your Chord Quest adventures in books 1 and 2.
2. Color in the badges on this pages as you think back on the lessons learned.

 For the first part of your test, review your powers on the left page and complete the challenges below.

PROVE YOUR:
- KNOWLEDGE
- PERFORMANCE SKILLS
- MEMORY

AND THEN...

YOU'LL HEAD TO THE SONGWRITING LAB!

2. PROVE YOUR KNOWLEDGE
BY ANSWERING THESE QUESTIONS...

What is Alberti bass?
_____ COMPLETE! ☐

What does it mean to "transpose" something?
_____ COMPLETE! ☐

What are some characteristics of Oom-Pah music?
_____ COMPLETE! ☐

3. PERFORM YOUR FAVORITE PIECE FROM THIS BOOK WITH ARTISTRY AND DYNAMICS

Title:
_____

Comments/Notes:
_____
_____
_____

COMPLETE! ☐

4. PLAY FROM MEMORY

Perform the I V vi IV progression with at least three different pattern combinations. It must be smooth and have style.

COMPLETE! ☐

Chord Quest Test

WELCOME TO THE SONGWRITING LAB!

For the next part of your test, follow the steps in the lab below.

Draw from the new skills and patterns you learned in this book!

Chord Quest Test

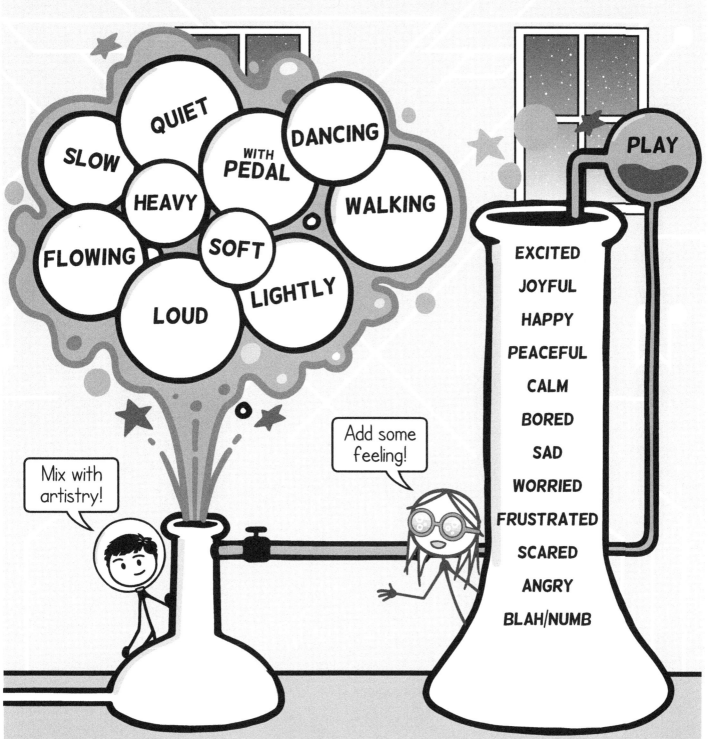

WRITE DOWN YOUR CREATIONS

Write down the creations and songs your created in the composer's lab here. You can include progressions, patterns, lyrics and more. Come back to the Songwriting Lab again and again to create more music!

NOW... BROADCAST YOUR CREATIVITY!
It's time to beam your creativity into the universe!

Take the song you wrote, or your favorite song from this book, and record it.

Did you find crystals throughout the book? Now they'll power your transponder and beam your creativity out into the universe!

TRANSMISSION TIME!

THE SONG I'VE CHOSEN TO RECORD:

_____

Choose the two (real life) people you want to send your recording to. It can be an audio recording of you playing your chosen song, or even better, a video!

WHO I'M SENDING MY RECORDING TO:

Person 1: _____ ☐ COMPLETE!

Person 2: _____ ☐ COMPLETE!

Next, transmit the signal. Send your recording to 2 (real life!) people, AND beam it to the Boring Book Factory!

It's working!

NO! My bots are breaking!

You've done it! Your creativity reached the factory and scrambled the signals of the machines! No more boring books!

Turn to page 84 for your award!

Your Creations

CHORD SCALE GLOSSARY

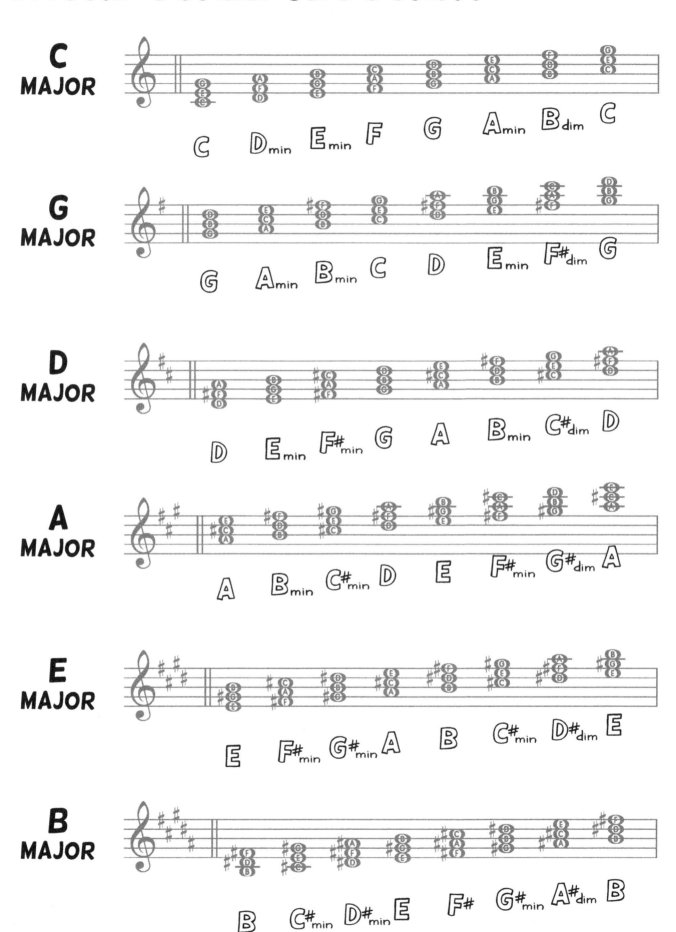

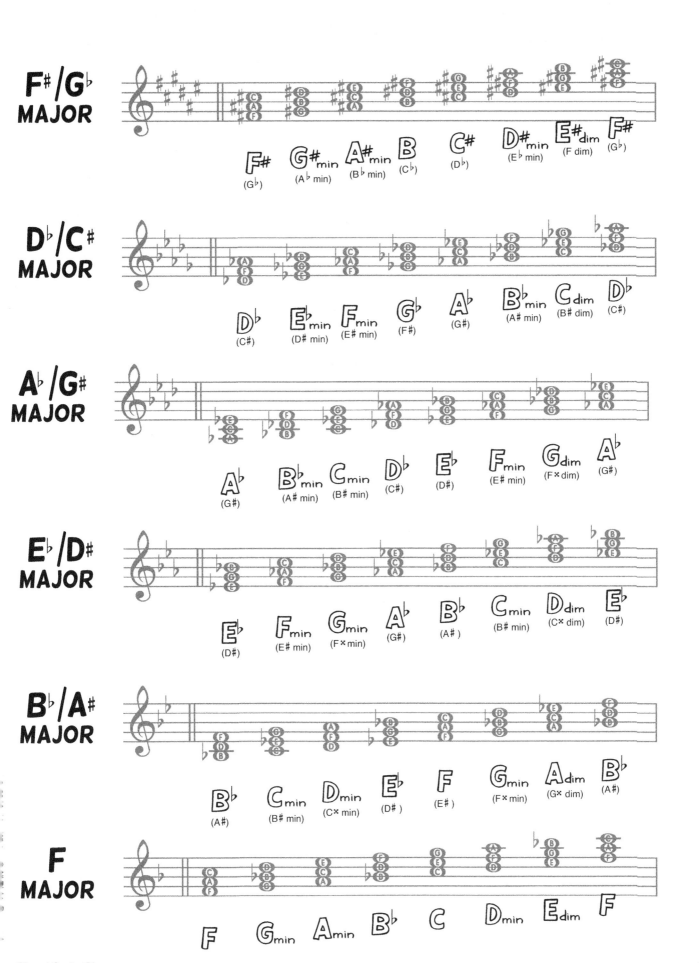

Now that you've completed Chord Quest Powerful Piano Lessons Level 2, let's take a look at what you'll learn next! Chord Quest Level 3 teaches many more great skills, such as:

- Inversions
- Rocking Chords
- Arpeggio Variations
- Syncopation
- One Four Five Progressions
- **And Much More!**

One of the most powerful skills learned in book 3 is inversions. Let's take a sneak peak at the first few pages of that chapter!

Sneak Peek

WHAT IS AN INVERSION?

THIS IS A CHORD IN ROOT POSITION

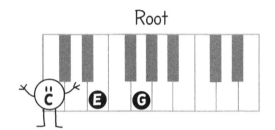

This is how you've been playing chords.

Root position is made up of stacked thirds. It looks like a snowman, don't you think? The name of the chord is the bottom note of the triad.

FIRST INVERSION

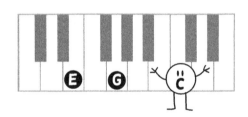

In first inversion, the root note is on the top of the chord.

SECOND INVERSION

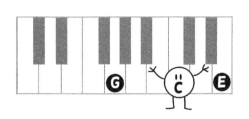

In second inversion, the root note is in the middle of the chord. It's a root note sandwich!

Using your right hand, play a C chord in root position, first inversion, second inversion, and root position again.

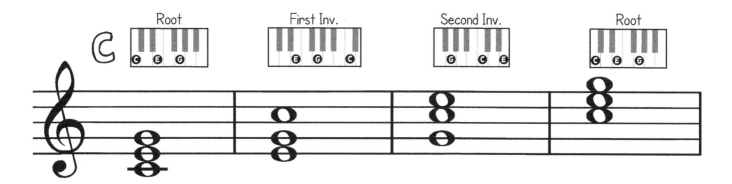

Now try arpeggio inversions with your right hand.

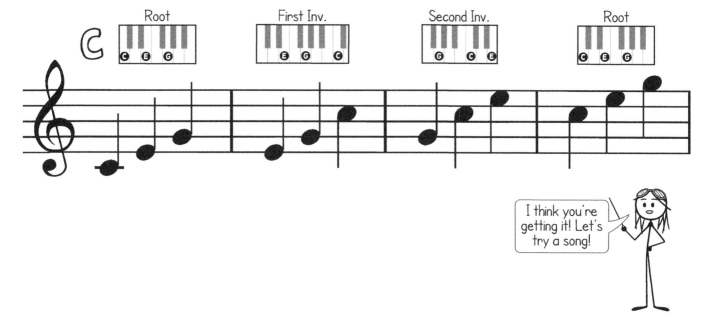

WITH OR WITHOUT INVERSIONS

ALL ROOT POSITION CHORDS

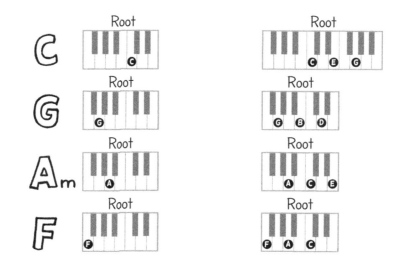

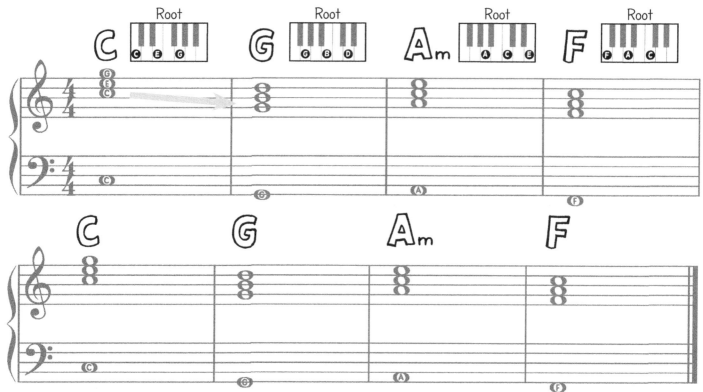

NOW LET'S TRY IT WITH AN INVERSION. JUST ONE CHANGE MAKES A BIG DIFFERENCE.

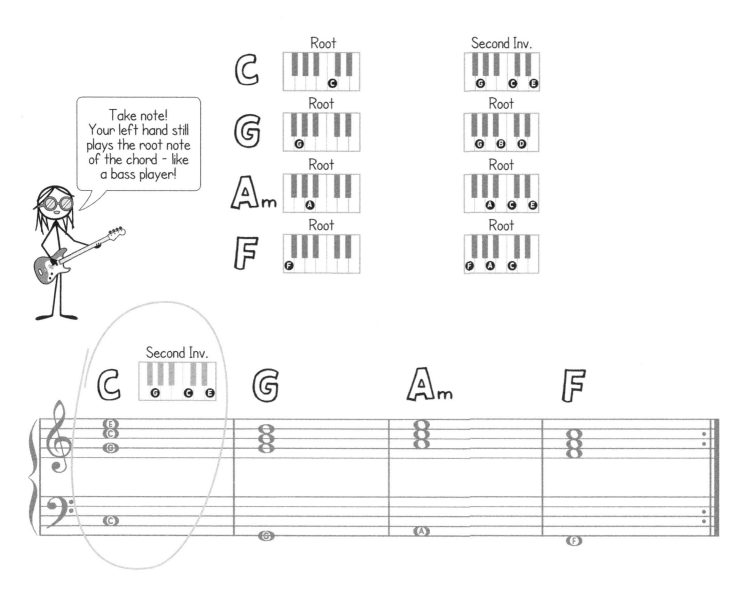

THE MERIDEE WINTERS MUSIC METHOD
Sparking brilliance with patterns, chords and games

Want to supercharge your progress with your instrument or find a tool to help you create music?
Find Meridee's globally-popular, trailblazing instructional books, innovative music games, online lesson info and more at merideewintersmusicmethod.com - or find us on Amazon.com!

YOUR NEXT QUEST!

CHORD QUEST SERIES

Our brains are wired to excel at patterns. Finally, a kid's music book that teaches that way. (And sure has fun doing it.)

What do you get when you take the great content and innovative teaching style from *Chord Crash Course*, but design and pace it for school aged kids? The *Chord Quest Powerful Piano Lessons* Series! Like its older counterpart, *Chord Quest* uses the power of patterns and shapes to have students playing great-sounding music from the very first lesson — without reading music. **Each book is its own quest where students learn universal patterns, earn powers and defeat villains like the Baron von Boring!**

PORTALS & POWERS

SUPER START! MY FIRST PIANO PATTERNS

Early childhood is a "magic window" for learning language – and young kids shouldn't wait to learn the language of music. "Super Start! My First Piano Patterns" teaches young beginners in the way their brains learn best – through patterns and play.

Super Start! My First Piano Patterns contains 36 piano pattern songs, games and activities that will guarantee a fun and successful start to piano lessons. As students work their way across Planet Plunk they learn, play, improvise, explore and even encounter a few "Plunkadillos." By using patterns, simple diagrams and playful characters, students sound great from day one – without needing to read music. Songs gradually increase in skill throughout the book, culminating in a final chapter of youngster-friendly waltzes and classically-inspired pattern songs. **Sound great! Play by shape!**

Meridee Winters Music Method ★ merideewintersmusicmethod.com

DEAR TRAILBLAZING TUNE-STERS,

WHETHER YOU'RE A TEACHER OR A LEARNER, WE HOPE YOU ARE ENJOYING YOUR MUSICAL ADVENTURES WITH CHORD QUEST!

IF YOU GET A CHANCE, PLEASE HELP US AND FUTURE MUSICAL LEARNERS BY WRITING A PRODUCT REVIEW. WE DEPEND HIGHLY ON YOUR FEEDBACK TO MAKE OUR CREATIVE MATERIALS THE BEST THEY CAN BE.

IF YOU ARE TEACHER WANTING TO CONNECT WITH OUR TEACHING COMMUNITY, OR A STUDENT WANTING TO CONNECT WITH A TEACHER, PLEASE CONTACT US AT BOOKS@MERIDEEWINTERS.COM OR 610-649-2782.

CREATIVELY YOURS,

Meridee Winters

P.S. – OUR ONLINE LESSONS ARE FOR KIDS OR ADULTS, AND WE HAVE A SPECIAL GIFT WAITING FOR YOU IF YOU MENTION THIS NOTE!

FUN FACT: WE READ ALL THE REVIEWS AND DO A LITTLE DANCE WHEN YOU WRITE ONE.

Join our creative, quirky community!

Made in the USA
Middletown, DE
21 October 2021